TiMe
for me

a burst of energy for busy women!

Helene Lerner

SOURCEBOOKS, INC.®
NAPERVILLE, ILLINOIS

Portions of this material excerpted from *Our Power As Women: Wisdom and Strategies of Highly
Successful Women*, by Helene Lerner, with permission of Conari Press, an imprint of Red
Wheel/Weiser, and *Stress Breakers* by Helene Lerner and Roberta Elins, formerly published by
Hazelden.

This publication is designed to provide accurate and authoritative information in regard to the
subject matter covered. It is sold with the understanding that the publisher is not engaged in
rendering legal, accounting, or other professional service. If legal advice or other expert
assistance is required, the services of a competent professional person should be sought.
—*From a Declaration of Principles Jointly Adopted by a Committee of the American Bar
Association and a Committee of Publishers and Associations*

Published by Sourcebooks, Inc.
P.O. Box 4410, Naperville, Illinois 60567-4410
(630) 961-3900
FAX: (630) 961-2168
www.sourcebooks.com

Library of Congress Cataloging-in-Publication Data
Lerner, Helene,
    Time for me : a burst of energy for busy women / by Helene Lerner.
        p. cm.
    1. Working mothers—United States—Life skills guides. 2. Work and
family—United States. 3. Women—Time management. 4. Stress management.
I. Title.

HQ759.48.L46 2005
158.1'085'2—dc22

2005003153

Printed and bound in Canada.
WC 10 9 8 7 6 5 4 3 2 1

For more information about the issues in *Time for Me* go to:
www.womenworking2000.com

Contents

Acknowledgments

Special thanks to Laura Epstein, Nubia DuVall, Anne-Marie McGintee, Meghan Harrington, Ellen Griffith, Lydia Wills, and Marcia Markland, who helped make *Time for Me* a reality, and to Deb Werksman at Sourcebooks, my wonderful editor and champion. Thanks also to all the wonderful women who shared their insights, feedback, and support, shaping the messages we know to be true but often forget.

Preface

It's so easy to get distracted by attending to everything and everybody around us that we often forget our own self-care, which we may or may not feel entitled to.

Among a woman's basic needs are food, clothing, shelter, passion, friendship, and fun.

Yes, fun! It lightens our burdens and gives us new perspectives. It frees our minds to face challenging situations, while knowing that we can handle anything that comes along.

Time for Me is written in two parts—the first part is a simple story about Ms. Owl's adventures. It is meant to charm, delight, and bring home profound insights that we all need to reflect upon. Part Two is a 4-step program to help you maintain your sparkle in everyday life.

Introduction: How I Came to Write This Book...

It's hard for me to confess this to you, but I know many of you will understand what I'm about to say. Did you ever look in the mirror and despite all the makeup you put on, something wasn't right? Well, that happened to me. When I looked at my face, although everything was the same, I noticed that my eyes had lost their sparkle.

As a woman, I wear many hats—TV host, executive producer, panel moderator, life-coach, author, mother, friend, and daughter. It makes me tired to name all of them! I'm a virtual doer, with very little time to just be (you know what I mean). Many people come to me for advice—I help busy women set their priorities straight. Unfortunately, I had forgotten the value of what I preach because I hadn't applied it to my own life.

I wrote this book to remind myself of what I already know— and was amused and recharged in the process. The central character you will meet is Ms. Owl. She is committed to moving ahead at work while raising her owlet, Oohie, whom she loves. The problem is that with all of her responsibilities, she's put herself last on the list for too long. And, as a result, she's lost that inner sparkle.

It was a delight for me to live vicariously through Ms. Owl's adventures. When I started to write this, I hadn't taken a much-needed vacation. Yet as I explored the fantasy of Ms. Owl's experiences at the Golden Nest Retreat Center, I was reenergized. In fact, after I wrote the book, I took some time off.

At the Golden Nest, Ms. Owl attends Quick Coach sessions, gets healing treatments, and meets some new friends. During her stay there, she has many realizations that change her life significantly. The practical wisdom in this book comes from the work I've done with women on assertiveness training, life-stage planning, and stress reduction. In Part Two, the 4-step program will help you gain perspective as you assess your priorities and goals.

I hope you enjoy reading *Time for Me* as much as I enjoyed writing it. But more important, the simple truths contained here are profound. If you take them to heart, they will change your life, too!

Part One:
A Fable of
the Modern-Day Woman

Ms. Owl and Her Dilemma

It was a dark winter's night with snow falling softly. Ms. Owl was perched on the top branch of the tree—working late as usual. All the other branches were empty because her coworkers had gone home. Once again, she was the only one left.

Her face appeared majestic in the moonlight. She had a few more gray feathers than when she had started at the company seasons ago, but her warm, friendly demeanor hadn't changed. She was proud to work for Owl USA, one of the oldest information providers, as an assistant to Boss Owl. Her willingness to help without complaining made her well liked by the male officers at the corporate roost.

But look more closely: she seemed tired—no, not tired—a bit sad. Something was wrong. A significant birthday was coming up in two days, and life felt bittersweet. She didn't feel like celebrating, even though she had a lot to be grateful for.

Back at her nest, she was raising Oohie, whom she adored. Unfortunately, her mate, Mr. Owl, wasn't home much, working the night shift at the airlines. So the brunt of the nest work fell on her. She tried to manage it all, but at what price? Her eyes had lost their sparkle.

As a female bird, she was notorious for putting herself last on the list—rarely taking time out for self-care. Although she did get her nails clipped every few weeks, it just wasn't enough. When was the last time she shared a meal with a friend to talk about frivolous things—like exotic migration spots, the latest store sales, or new reads for a rainy day?
She was about to call it a night—pack up and fly home—when she looked under her briefcase and saw an envelope. *Just one more piece of mail to handle,* she thought.

The Invitation

She took the envelope in her beak and opened it. To her surprise, inside was a card that read:

Free Weekend At the
Golden Nest

March 5th to 8th

AN Admirer

Who could have given this to her? She really had no idea. She had heard about the Golden Nest, a new retreat center. It was supposed to be wonderful. The gift was intriguing, but how could she get away? Mr. Owl was on assignment until the seventh. Who would take care of Oohie? The day after she got back she had a presentation due for Boss Owl, so when would she prepare her report?

But something inside her said, "*Go*. Everything will fall into place." It was unlike her to be so impetuous, but she decided to do it.

Everything *did* fall into place—her best friend, the falcon next door, agreed to look after the little one. And even though he wouldn't be around, Mr. Owl encouraged her to go.

The Golden Nest

Ms. Owl started off on her journey. She flew south for several hours into a welcome change of weather. The sun warmed her petite frame as she glided through the air. She could already feel herself relaxing and there was no question in her mind it was exciting to be getting away.

It was late afternoon when she arrived at the gate that surrounded the Golden Nest. A sign posted at the entrance read: *The Golden Nest: Dedicated to Your Creative Expansion.* It was a lovely place. There was a lake on the property with a beautiful shimmering fountain. All sorts of birds were perched on the branches of tall trees circling the lake.

Taking a deep breath, she felt a sense of calm. This would be her home for the next three days. She smiled a big smile and felt her wing muscles relax. It was good to be here!

Just then, a white heron flew over, eager to greet the new guest: "Hi there. Here's where you dine," she said, gesturing to a grand old tree. "You must go to the Quick Coach seminars after meals. There you will reflect on your life, and what you'd like to change about it. That's the purpose of the retreat. You'll also have free use of the facility and a few treatments. I suggest you get a feather massage. Be sure to explore the gardens too. The flowers are starting to bloom." Then the heron flew off.

It was with a mixture of trepidation and elation that Ms. Owl faced the weekend. She wasn't used to focusing on herself, and didn't know what to expect. She dined and retired to her resting tree for the night.

The Majestic Eagle

Ms. Owl awoke to the sweet sounds of the other birds and a magnificent view—the sun was rising, painting the sky in shades of pink and gold.

She had a bite to eat and went straight to the Quick Coach seminar. The Gilded Perch was already packed with other birds—all were eager for the session to begin. Ms. Owl didn't know anyone and felt awkward. She was beginning to have second thoughts about whether this was right for her. All of a sudden, a brown-and-gray-feathered eagle swooped down to the perch. She fanned her tail feathers and strutted to the front of the crowd with confidence. She looked directly at the birds.

"Many of you have come here to recharge yourself and get your sparkle back. You'll do that by taking a good look at situations that get you off track. I'll give you strategies to handle these challenges. But the real trick is keeping your sparkle when you get back home. I encourage you to make friends here because they will be a great resource for you when you return."

Ms. Owl felt the stirrings of hope. She had been running on empty for weeks. It pained her that she no longer felt enthusiastic about work or even about being with Oohie. *That's exactly it: my life has no sparkle*, she thought.

The eagle set some ground rules. "If you have something to say, say it. And be as truthful as possible. Your contribution is important."

It wasn't at all like Ms. Owl to start first, but her anxiety compelled her to. She blurted out nervously, "You've put your finger on it exactly! I want to feel excited about my life again. Much of the time, I feel exhausted."

The eagle responded, "You are aware of the problem; that is key!" And she wrote on a white board balanced in a convenient notch in the tree:

*Knowing that
      there is an imbalance
            in your life
      is the first step toward
            changing it.*

"Let's talk about a typical day at work, and the things that distract you," she continued.

The responses tumbled out:

"A coworker comes over and says, 'You have to help with this.' I do it and then don't have time to finish my own project," complained Ms. Owl.

"Other birds constantly interrupt me with trivial things," called out an egret.

"Gossip," squawked a heron. "I love it, but after indulging, my work piles up."

"Lots of honesty," said the coach. "Everything you just described keeps the focus off of *you* and depletes your energy. Here, you'll learn new ways. At the Golden Nest, you don't have to attend to anyone but yourself."

She went to the board and scrawled:

*M*ake self-care a priority!

"Remember this during your stay. Now, it's time to explore the property and get to know each other. You're free 'til the next meeting."

Given the cue, the birds went off. As Ms. Owl left the gilded perch, she realized how limited her life had become—when did she have time to laugh with a friend, squawk at each other's jokes? She couldn't remember the last time she had gone dancing with Mr. Owl. They used to love strutting around the clubs. Now Ms. Owl was more agitated than when she had arrived. She was being asked to take a hard look at herself. Was she up to the task?

Ms. Owl didn't feel like mixing with the other birds, so she flew around the grounds alone. Her mind was racing, trying to figure out why life was so stressful.

Just then, she noticed that it was nearing ten o'clock, time for the feather massage she had signed up for the night before. She went off to find the Golden Table—the place where all the treatments were done.

Ms. Owl had never had a massage before and felt a little uncomfortable at first. Robin, a bird with soft eyes and a soothing manner took her to a special spot and wrapped a satin cloth around her, putting Ms. Owl at ease.

Robin hummed a sweet tune as she stroked Ms. Owl's feathers with her healing beak, and Ms. Owl started to relax. It was wonderful to have someone attend to *her* for a change.

After the session was over, Robin gave Ms. Owl some lovely mint water and invited her to perch for a bit. What a luxury, not having to rush to another meeting or appointment. Robin stayed to chat for a while. Ms. Owl was touched by her generosity.

The eagle waited for the birds to settle into their seats before beginning Session Two. As soon as the room quieted down, she started, "Many of you aren't as joyful as you would like to be. While you're here, you will be reminded of pleasurable activities that now take a backseat to your other responsibilities. Don't dismay. You can choose to bring them back."

"Let's start with a rule of thumb. *Your joy quotient needs to be about 50 percent each day.* Yes, 50 percent, no less. A 50 percent joy quotient means you feel positive 50 percent of your waking time. This may seem like a lot, but it's not."

Ms. Owl was put off by the percentages, thinking, *50 percent…I'd be lucky with 25 percent—and these days, 10 percent.* She spoke up. "Back home, I'm so overscheduled that I've forgotten why I became involved in activities." Lots of the other birds nodded their heads in agreement. Ms. Owl was certainly not alone.

The eagle responded by writing on the board:

*W*hy you want
to achieve a goal
is more important
than actually attaining it.

"Most of the goals we've set for ourselves have come and gone. But why we want them—what we think they will bring us—never changes. What is that for you?" she asked the group.

The birds reflected and then called out:

"Influence."

"Respect from other birds."

"Go deeper," said the eagle.

"Being content with myself."

"Happiness."

"Yes, we've lost sight of these aspirations because we are too focused on achievement. Give this some thought today." And with that, the eagle ended the session.

Ms. Owl admitted to herself that she had accomplished a lot over the last decade, but hadn't really enjoyed her success. The frenetic pace of her life didn't allow her to appreciate the gifts that she had. The enormity of the changes she would have to make to live in a balanced way overwhelmed her. She decided to go to the resting tree for a nap.

Instead of feeling refreshed, Ms. Owl awoke depressed. There was no place to go, nothing she *had* to do. She couldn't hide her feelings in activity. She took a look at a pamphlet all the birds were given when they arrived at the Golden Nest, "It's Your Life, So What Are You Going to Do with It?" It talked about getting off the treadmill and creating the future as you would like it to be. It asked how satisfied she was with her job and family life. What changes was she willing to make? It was difficult for her to answer these questions, but it got her thinking.

The clock chimed on the hour. It was time for a guided tour of the gardens. She didn't really feel like going, but pushed herself to fly off to the big oak tree where all were gathering.

The flock took off. The colors below were dazzling and Ms. Owl felt more at ease. The gardens reminded her of times spent as an owlet collecting flower petals with her mother. But with this good feeling came a tinge of sadness. How long had it been since she had done something just for fun?

Lady

At dinner, Ms. Owl perched next to Lady, a beautiful sparrow. Lady had migrated from England a few years ago after going through a divorce. Life as a single parent in the States wasn't easy. Her mother had come over with them and took care of her little one while Lady was working.

Ms. Owl found that she and Lady had a lot in common. They shared many of the same concerns, even though their lives seemed so different. Whatever else came out of the retreat, she had found a new friend.

It was a few minutes until their next meeting, so they flew off into the starry night. When they arrived at the Gilded Perch, the eagle was asking the group if anyone had any questions.

Ms. Owl decided that this was her chance to talk about something that was bothering her. "Saying no is so hard for me. I keep helping others even when I have little to give."

The coach responded, "You can't give what you don't have, so you need to nurture yourself first. Isn't that true?"

Ms. Owl nodded in agreement. The other birds fell silent, lost in their own thoughts. They wanted to do that, but it didn't come naturally. They weren't used to taking time for themselves.

The eagle then wrote on the board:

Saying "no" is like saying "yes" to yourself.

She went on, "It may seem selfish at first, but it isn't—it's self-care." Then the eagle picked Lady and Ms. Owl for a role-play—prompting them on how to respond. Lady pretended to ask Ms. Owl for help on a project. Ms. Owl deliberated and answered that she could give her a hand next week, but not right now.

The group talked about how Ms. Owl was able to set limits by defining what she could and could not do. She took a moment to think about the request and not answer immediately. She had more than just the two choices "yes" or "no," and had found another solution.

Next, the eagle handed out a diary to each bird and asked them to write down special things that they would like to do for themselves in the weeks to come. They spent about fifteen minutes making their lists and then took a ten-minute break to talk to each other.

Lady and Ms. Owl talked about how difficult it was going to be to set limits back home, but what it would be like if they could.

"I'd have time to sing with other birds. Before I moved to this country, I would get together with a group once a week," said Lady wistfully.

Just then, the eagle called them back. Tonight was an extended session. Ms. Owl whispered to Lady,

"You must find time to sing when you return home. It's essential to your happiness!"

The eagle began, "Tell me about your relationships. Female birds have a tendency to do more than their fair share. Do you give more than you receive?"

Lady spoke up: "I take on more than I should. I feel like I have to prove myself." Ms. Owl thought about Mr. Owl and her male coworkers. They expected her to do the brunt of the work. And all these years she had gone along with it. She didn't know another way. "How can we stop doing that?" she squawked.

"Don't do the extras," directed the coach. "By not doing them, you're effectively assigning those tasks to the other birds."

She wrote on the board:

> *P*ick the tasks
> you want to do
>   and have time for—
> and leave the rest.

The eagle went on, "With any imbalance, you can initiate change. Drop the rope and take a wait-and-see attitude. You'll be surprised at the results."

Ms. Owl wasn't convinced, and mumbled to Lady, "What if the other bird doesn't take on more?"

Lady responded, "I know what you mean."

It was getting late, and the eagle ended the meeting.

Ms. Owl had a restless night thinking about how she would change things back home. She simply didn't know if she could. And what would happen if she did? Certainly, it would cause tension with Mr. Owl.

She had made plans to meet Lady before breakfast. Lady greeted her with a welcoming smile, and they took off together for a brisk flight around the lake.

The water below was sparkling in the sunlight, and the peaceful surroundings gave her comfort. She wanted to believe that things would work out, even if she didn't know how.

The new friends shared a quick breakfast, and then flew over to the Gilded Perch for their next coaching session.

The Gilded Perch

he eagle began, "I want to acknowledge your courage, your willingness to look at the root of your problems. That's how change happens. Let's start with an exercise that you can use in times of stress."

"Close your eyes and listen closely to the sounds of the Gilded Perch."

There was an instant hush as the birds closed their eyes.

"Can you hear the wind whistling, the faint buzzing of the insects, a feather rustling? I want you to go beyond these sounds and listen more intently."

After about twenty seconds, they opened their eyes. The coach asked for reactions. One of the birds said, "That was so peaceful, like being suspended in time."

"Yes. At any moment of your day, you have the power to stop what you are doing and *pause*, just as we did just now."

She scrawled on the board:

*P*ause
between activities.

"Now," the eagle continued, "Let's focus on your sparkle. Where do you think it comes from?"

The birds offered:

"From feeling good about myself."

"From having a sense of well-being."

"That's right," said the coach. "Pruning and dyeing your feathers may help, but that doesn't create sparkle. How you feel about yourself, the joy you experience at any given moment, what you are passionate about—that makes you charismatic."

Ms. Owl said, "I'm not sure what I feel passionate about anymore." She was not alone. There were others in the group who felt the same way.

The eagle directed, "I want each of you to answer three questions and share what you discover with a partner."

"First question: What makes your heart sing?"

"Second question: What is something you loved to do as a young bird but you no longer do?"

"Third question: Who in your life makes your feathers green with envy? Think about why. What are these birds accomplishing that you aren't?"

Ms. Owl told Lady about how she had collected flower petals when she was little. She and her mother would take them back to their nest and make magnificent arrangements. Ms. Owl didn't have time anymore for something so frivolous. Instead, she envied her friends who were decorating their nests.

Lady spoke again about her desire to sing with a group, recalling fond memories of early morning songs. "We have to bring these pleasures back into our lives."

The eagle summoned the birds together and offered some final remarks. "What you are passionate about doesn't have to be grand. It can be simple activities that give you pleasure. Don't waste time on jealousy or envy. Start doing the things you enjoy. I'll see you after dinner."

Ms. Owl's heart was opening. Her spirit had been reawakened, and there was a definite glow about her. She was developing a new habit—pampering herself.

She wanted to be alone to digest the events of the morning and went off to fly around the lake, getting a quick bite after that.

She contemplated signing up for a body scrub with feather fluffing in the afternoon. Ms. Owl told herself she deserved the treatment, half believing it. Dare she do it? Of course she should, and so she did. She looked dazzling when it was all finished. Simply divine!

There was a short meeting after dinner. The eagle wanted to arm the birds with strategies to deal with criticism—something that they would likely be up against at home, especially when they started to take more time for themselves. The coach's words shifted their thinking: "Criticism is all around us, and it can be very destructive. Simply take what fits, and leave the rest! When a bird strikes out, it's usually about himself, not you. Best to forgive—he's really crying out for help, but he doesn't know it."

The eagle scrawled on the board:

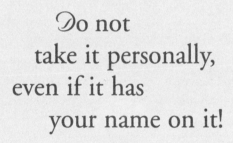

Do not
take it personally,
even if it has
your name on it!

After the session ended, Ms. Owl flew to the Mystic Branch Café before retiring for the night. There was a bird in resplendent feathers reading parrot cards in the far corner. She waited her turn and when it came, the seer announced that good fortune was coming her way, even though the specifics weren't apparent.

He advised Ms. Owl to make sure to connect with her new friends from the Golden Nest once she got back home. They would encourage her to use her power wisely: "The future will take care of itself. There are many gifts for you here, right now! Focus on the present."

She couldn't leave without asking if he knew the gift-giver responsible for her stay at the Golden Nest.

He turned over a few more cards, but came up empty. She'd have to solve that mystery on her own.

When Ms. Owl awoke the next morning, she realized that this was her last full day at the Golden Nest. A part of her didn't want to leave. She missed her family but certainly didn't miss the stress of her daily routine. She made sure that she remembered to exchange business crackers with Lady and some of the other lovely birds she had met during her stay.

Ms. Owl would make every effort to stay in touch with her new friends, especially with Lady. This was more than a friendship; both birds would need to be support buddies when they returned home. And she wouldn't let this relationship slide. The two met for a quick breakfast and then went to the Gilded Perch.

It was the final session of the weekend. Several birds were anxious about leaving. The eagle was used to last-day tension and said, "Change is not easy. When you go back, you must stay in touch— your 'sister' birds will encourage you to take the right actions."

She then passed out small notepads for phone numbers and b-mail addresses and gave them time to mill around and collect each other's contact information.

The eagle called the group back together again. "We've talked about relationships. I'd like to focus on the most important relationship of all, the one you have with yourself. What gets in the way of your feeling satisfied and happy?"

Ms. Owl offered, "Perfectionism does me in. I know we all make mistakes, but I can't seem to accept it when I do."

"That was true for me too," commented a pelican, "but I'm getting a better handle on this. My mentor helped me realize that I couldn't control everything. She asked me the following question: 'If you are at the beach and a wave comes at you, can you push it back?' Of course I can't, but I was acting as if I could, demanding extraordinary things of myself. She said, 'You are as bound to make mistakes as a wave is to complete itself.' I realized that what was constraining me was not the mistakes, but my trying to control not making mistakes. As long as I am conscious of my mistakes and learn from them—try not to make them again—that is enough!"

Agreeing with the pelican, the coach wrote on the board:

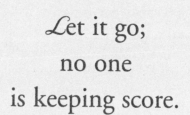

*L*et it go;
no one
is keeping score.

Ms. Owl wanted to thank the pelican personally for the comment. It resonated deeply within her.

She had tried to cover her tracks so many times. Only now did she come to a sudden realization— what was the worst thing that could happen if she made a mistake? Whatever it was, it wasn't as bad as what she thought it would be. The weekend had helped Ms. Owl take a larger view of life, and in that context, mistakes didn't really matter.

The eagle complimented the group for their tenacity and said, "A good practice for you to take back home and use in times of stress is the *60-second inventory*. At any time during the day, just stop what you are doing and ask yourself: 'How do I feel? What's bothering me and why am I holding on to it? What do I have to be grateful for?' And if you need to, call one of your 'sister' birds and share your insights with her. That will help you get back on track."

Their time together was drawing to a close. Although they did not want the session to end, it would have to. Knowing that, the birds nuzzled together and exchanged their good-byes.

As they left the perch, the coach gave them a final gift. It was a pamphlet titled "Inner Upkeep," filled with reflections and exercises that they could practice back at home.

Ms. Owl met Lady to get their final treatment, a luxurious lavender birdbath. They flew together to a small pond on the property.

The ground around the water was filled with purple flowers and the smell of lavender permeated the air. Although it felt extravagant, they relished these last few minutes of self-indulgence. It helped soothe their sadness about leaving. They vowed to make reservations and come back next year.

Going Home

L ater that night, Ms. Owl started the trip back to her nest. The moonlight lit the way and her face sparkled as she glided through the night sky. Ms. Owl began to feel anxious as she thought of her return, and went over the weekend's lessons to calm herself:

- Knowing that there is an imbalance in my life is the first step toward changing it.
- Make self-care a priority.
- My "joy" quotient needs to be at least 50 percent each day.
- Why I want to achieve a goal is more important than actually attaining it.
- I can't give away what I don't have.
- Saying "no" is like saying "yes" to myself.
- Stop doing the extras—others will pick up the slack.
- Pause between activities.

- Do not take it personally, even if it has my name on it.
- Let it go; nobody is keeping score.

The flight went by quickly and it seemed that she was home in no time. As she neared the nest, Oohie spotted her and flew her way, cooing joyously. Mr. Owl was there, too. They were all happy to be reunited.

After spending some time together catching up, the family retired for the night. Before going to sleep, Mr. Owl confessed that it was he who had given her the Golden Nest weekend. He planned it several months ago and wanted it to be intriguing, so he didn't identify himself.

Ms. Owl was filled with appreciation. She stroked his beak and they fluffed each other's feathers. This was the moment, she thought, to express her needs. She took a risk and told him that he would have to pitch in more around the nest. She had simply been doing too much.

Mr. Owl became defensive. Ms. Owl's heart was pounding. She didn't know what to say, so she said nothing. A few minutes passed and Mr. Owl hooted, "I do some of the errands around here…" but he didn't continue. There was an uncomfortable silence. Both knew there would be changes and that it wouldn't be easy.

Ms. Owl learned something that night: it was more risky not to say anything because then she would be living a lie. And she didn't want to do that anymore.

The Corporate Roost

Ms. Owl awoke from a restless sleep thinking about work. She looked over her notes in preparation for the report she would be presenting to her supervisor, Boss Owl. She was edgy about the meeting, and wanted to be as well-prepared as possible.

Arriving at Owl USA, she flew directly to the conference branch where the group was gathering. The office staff were there looking crisp in their pinstriped vests. It was a conservative group—a good-old-bird network. She was fond of most of them, with the exception of a young sprout, Jon, a know-it-all who really annoyed her.

Boss Owl called the meeting to order and said, "I want to announce that the Bulk Sales Division is coming under our wing. Ms. Owl, you will report to me as usual but take on the added role as associate supervisor overseeing the division."

Ms. Owl hadn't expected this and was amazed by her reaction: "I'd be glad to take on added responsibilities, but I will need an assistant." This was not like her; she usually said "yes" without asking for help, and suffered the consequences later on.

"Very well, Jon will be available to you temporarily. But I don't know how long you'll have him for." Ms. Owl figured that it was better to have him on board than not to have anyone. She'd deal with his replacement later. She was smiling inside. Her stay at the Golden Nest was already paying off. Ms. Owl gave her report and the meeting ended.

When she got back to her branch, she b-mailed Lady right away and told her what had happened. Lady b-mailed back, "Way to go, gal, but you're guaranteed to have some bumpy times ahead."

Enjoying this small victory, Ms. Owl was aware that there would be challenges in the months to come but she now had friends to support her along the way. She had learned the importance of putting herself first, and that no one could take her sparkle unless she gave it away. She vowed never to do that again.

Epilogue

here was a long weekend coming up. As usual, I wasn't sure if I could get away but I knew I really needed to. My son Heath was taken care of—between basketball games, movies, and appointments with friends, his schedule was set. My assistant was more than capable of following up on any pressing business. (Isn't it amazing how indispensable we feel sometimes?) Really, there was no excuse not to take some time off. I just had to change gears and book my trip, so I did.

I went to a retreat center in Massachusetts where I have gone before to recharge. The grounds are beautiful. There are mountains surrounding the property, and you can see a wonderful lake from the main house.

When I walked inside to register, I felt my body starting to relax. I was surprised to meet an acquaintance of mine I hadn't seen in years. She had been staying there, too. Later that afternoon we met to catch up. She told me that an old mentor of ours lived nearby. She had her phone number, so of course I called her. We planned to meet for lunch on Sunday. Needless to say, things were working out even better than I had planned.

The next morning, I walked down to the lake and was struck by how glorious everything looked. I took a path through the woods to get there and the birds were squawking loudly. I thought of Ms. Owl and smiled.

The lake was very still that day. The sun was sparkling on it and the water shimmered. I took some deep breaths and felt grateful to be alive. In the afternoon, I had a massage and was amazingly relaxed. When I put my head to the pillow that night, I sank into a deep sleep, which was unusual for me.

What a wonderful gift I had given myself—time to nourish my mind, body, and soul. After focusing on my self-care, I'm sure you can guess what happened. My "sparkle" came back.

Part Two:
How to Make Time for Me

I've created a 4-step program to help you *carve out time* to maintain your sparkle. There will be questionnaires to fill out and exercises for you to follow. As you go through the steps, share insights you receive with a supportive friend or colleague.

The Journey Continues…

his 4-step program, with exercises, reflections, and practical advice, is designed to help you act differently in situations that can deplete your energy.

For example, many of us demand too much of ourselves and are perfectionists. We may find it hard to say "no," and feel guilty when we do. We often have a difficult time with criticism. In Step One, you will fill out a questionnaire and "get clear" about why you are not as fulfilled as you would like to be. You will be encouraged to take risks in order to change this.

Step Two will help you let go of ways of acting that do not serve you. You'll become aware of impediments that keep you stuck, and be given the tools to move on.

In Step Three, you will uncover and explore your passions, committing to activities where the sole purpose is pleasing yourself. (Yes, you are entitled to that, and you're not being selfish!)

Finally, Step Four offers daily reflections that will enable you to flex your "inner" muscles. I'll ask you to keep a log of activities that puts into practice valuable insights from this book.

As you start the process, you will undoubtedly feel some fear. Why shouldn't you? You are in uncharted territory. But don't let that distract you. I encourage you to take action anyway. Keep focused on your goal: to lead a more joyful and fulfilling life.

Step One: Get Clear

Awareness is the first step toward changing, so I want you to answer the following questions honestly. If uncomfortable emotions come up as you do this, that's to be expected. Endorse yourself for being willing to take a look at what keeps you stuck. You may want to share what you've discovered with a supportive friend.

1. Which of your daily tasks feel mechanical and routine?

_____

_____

_____

_____

_____

2. What dreams have you put on hold because you feel your day-to-day responsibilities should take priority?

_____

_____

_____

_____

3. If money were not a concern, how would you be spending your time? What career, hobbies, or activities would you be actively involved in?

_____

_____

_____

_____

4. When you were a child, what things excited you—caused you to get up in the morning, looking forward to the day?

_____

_____

_____

_____

5. What makes you feel most joyful now?

_____

_____

_____

_____

6. If you knew you had one year to live, what would you change about your life?

_____

_____

_____

_____

7. Regarding your personal and professional dreams, what do you think is possible for you to achieve? Impossible to achieve?

_____

_____

_____

_____

8. You may feel guilty about living richly and fully. Why do you think that is? What other beliefs do you have about yourself that may be impeding your growth?

_____

_____

_____

_____

9. Are you a perfectionist? Explain.

_____

_____

_____

_____

10. Upon receiving criticism, do you judge yourself harshly?

_____

_____

_____

_____

11. Do you have difficulty saying "no" when someone asks you to help out, even if you're already too busy? What stops you from saying "no"?

_____

_____

_____

_____

12. Are you a procrastinator? Explain.

_____

_____

_____

_____

13. Create your network. Who will support you in moving forward? Make a list of people you can count on. What would you ask from each person? For example, it's a useful practice to call someone before and after you take a risk.

_____

_____

_____

_____

As you proceed through the steps, take risks and try new things. I support you to take action toward achieving goals that you may not feel able or entitled to reach. Do not give up. Go for it! If fear surfaces, let it, but realize there is no guarantee that something negative won't happen, even during routine activities. So you might as well take a chance on something that can transform your life.

And after you keep doing what you thought was risky, it becomes second nature. Think of your first day at your current job or how you felt when you found out you were going to be a mom—all those changes involved risk, but you did them. Now going to work and taking care of the kids seems so natural. When you step out in a new way, you're bound to feel uncomfortable. It's important to honor this discomfort because it means that you are changing. In fact, if you keep pressing on, you may find that your fear turns into excitement.

Step Two: Let Go

This step will help you shed habits that you may have outgrown but are afraid to let go of, like perfectionism, not being able to say "no," an oversensitivity toward criticism, and procrastination. Discarding them will not be easy because you've probably been acting this way for a long time. But with the tools you'll learn here, you can start to take more nurturing actions for yourself.

As you begin, you're bound to make mistakes along the way. Don't get discouraged; rather, keep moving forward as if your new mindset is one that you've had for awhile. Remind yourself that your goal is to create more joy in your life. Like physical exercise, building muscles (in this case, "inner" muscles) involves growing pains, which will ultimately go away the more you practice.

We are so used
to feeling under pressure that
we believe stress is a
normal part of everyday life.

But the truth is,
we are stressed because
we are "stressable."
It's not the situations in
our lives that cause us stress
but our reactions to them.

Perfectionism

Are you a perfectionist? Answer the following questions and find out. Think of how you've handled specific situations as you respond.

- Do you set unusually high standards for yourself and others and get disappointed if they are not met?
- Are you rarely satisfied after you have accomplished a task, not giving yourself the credit you deserve or looking to achieve something else?
- Do you lose perspective easily, treating a minor task as important as a major one—thinking that everything has to be done perfectly?
- Are you overly sensitive to criticism and dwell on it even after the moment has passed?

All of your answers may not be clear-cut, but if you lean towards saying "yes" to any of them, then— like most of us—you are probably a perfectionist. Perfectionism is usually riddled with the fear that you will be judged harshly if you don't do something the "right" way.

With women's late entry into the workforce, we've had to prove ourselves on the job, often having to be twice as good as our male counterparts. And if we don't measure up to this exaggerated standard (who could?), we are made to—or make ourselves—feel inadequate. Let's help each other to stop doing that. We do more than our "fair share" as it is, more than adequately. Besides, no one is keeping score!

Here are some strategies to help you change your perspective and treat yourself more kindly:

- Before you engage in an activity, think positively. Tell yourself that you are about to embark on a task that will be completed in a timely and efficient manner, even if it isn't done perfectly.
- When you make a mistake, don't dwell on it. Look at how you could have done things differently and move on. Think to yourself, next!
- Endorse yourself when you do something out of the ordinary. (For example, tell yourself, "Way to go, girl!" when you make time during the week to have dinner with friends.)

Exercise: Think Positively

If you feel yourself tensing up because your mind is racing with negative thoughts, *stop* whatever you are doing. Sit quietly and become aware of your body and what you are telling yourself. For example, my mouth is dry, I feel tightness in my throat, I am thinking that my report is not good enough. Now, calm yourself by affirming that what you are doing is more than adequate, and that you have the time and energy to complete the task successfully.

Criticism

It's as harmful to your well-being as perfectionism. For example, a coworker belittles your performance at a meeting and your feelings of inadequacy are triggered. Although you try to not let this bother you, you feel defensive, thinking, *She has no business criticizing me because she's not my supervisor.* Her comments most likely stem from her own insecurity and may or may not be related to any-thing you've done. The lesson here: Take what fits and leave the rest! Your priority is to be gracious toward yourself.

Exercise: Pause

Next time someone strikes out at you, breathe deeply and don't react immediately. If it's appropriate to assert yourself, do. Say how you feel, using an "I" statement. For example, "I feel uncomfortable because you brought that up in front of my boss." When you've said what you needed to, let it go. After all, you've judged your fair share of people too.

And when you are about to criticize someone, *pause*! Examine why you feel agitated. Is it because of what he or she is doing? Or are you reminded of something that you haven't wanted to face about yourself? Truth: What you think or say about others is often a reflection of how you feel about yourself. So be mindful of your words. They have power and shape your reality. If you are finding fault with people, they feel judged and insecure. If you are loving and supportive, they feel safe and confident.

Now, not all criticism is harmful. For example, honest feedback is one of the greatest gifts you can receive because it is given with the intention of helping you grow, so you don't want to push it away. To tell the difference between criticism and honest feedback, just look into the person's eyes and you'll know if the remark is said with caring.

Exercise: Reflect

When someone gives you feedback, repeat what's been said and acknowledge that you have understood it. Although you may be feeling defensive, say nothing additional. For example, to your boss you might say, "On the whole you are pleased with my performance, but I've made quite a few mistakes lately on the client's weekly report and I need to proofread my work better." Or to your teenage daughter, "You are angry because I've missed the last two soccer games. And I must go to the one coming up." Repeating a comment gives you the space to reflect on it, before saying something you'll regret later on.

Saying "No"

Have you ever agreed to do something just because you were afraid of a disapproving reaction if you declined? In other words, you didn't feel entitled to say "no." Turning someone down is still a challenge for many of us. We want to please others because we want to be liked. But we simply can't be all things to all people.

Saying "no" can be positive
when it frees you to do what is
most beneficial for you and others.

Saying "yes" too many times
may mean that you're trying to
seduce others into liking you
by being who *they* want you to be.
Have faith that they will like you
even better for who you are.

And if they don't,
you may need to move on.

How can we get a handle on saying "no"? We need to evaluate new requests for our help with the existing commitments we have, then make a choice based upon what seems most important at the moment. In other words, if you say "yes" to a request, you most likely will have to let another commitment go, rather than do both.

Take this scenario. Someone asks you to assist at the company picnic, which involves helping to plan the event as well as staffing a table that day. Ask yourself: *What will I have to give up in order to do this? Will taking this on better suit my needs?* You may say "yes" because it's an opportunity to meet new people and be visible in the department. If you do, you will have to tell a coworker that you can't assist with his project any longer. You may want to help him look for a replacement.

Here's another example. Your boss asks you to participate in a meeting which conflicts with your child's piano recital. If you consider the meeting to be relatively unimportant, you've just finished working on a report that required overtime, and you've spent time away from your family, tell your boss, "I can't be there." However, if the meeting is with the head of the division and it would be important for you to attend, you may decide differently. Grandparents or your significant other can cover for you at the performance, but under no circumstances can you miss the next one.

Likewise, "no" is appropriate if you've just come home from a family vacation, you're tired and a little under the weather, and your significant other wants you to go bowling with friends. If his response is less than enthusiastic when you turn him down, hold your ground—even if you feel a bit guilty or angry when you do.

Each situation demanding your time calls for a unique response. For instance, if you haven't seen each other much lately and he wants to spend quality time together, it's important to find a way to do that.

Exercise: Practice Makes Perfect

The more you practice saying "no," the easier it will get. Think about a situation with your boss, husband, child, or friend that you should have declined, but didn't. It could be anything from a dinner invitation to helping out with a project. Now picture yourself doing it differently. How would circumstances have changed if you said "no" or "not right now"?

Delegating

One reason that it's been difficult to say "no" is that we want tasks to be done right, meaning *our way*! (There's our perfectionism again.) And we don't like giving up control. As a result, we spread ourselves too thin. But as we've seen, doing it all yourself doesn't allow you to fully address the important activities—the ones only you can do or want to do.

By delegating, you get the majority of the work done and share the experience with others. At work, try to give away tasks that don't require your minute-to-minute involvement. If you're at home with your child, let him or her put away the laundry. So what if the towels aren't folded exactly your way? The chore is completed and your child feels good about helping.

Now, what happens if you ask someone to help out and he doesn't? How do you handle that? Here's a suggestion: *Drop the rope.* Just don't do the task, and see what happens. For example, you ask your teenage son to clean up his room, and he doesn't. Don't you do it; just close his door, and let him live in the "mess." Or you've asked your mate to pick up some juice and he doesn't. He may change his mind when he's thirsty and there's nothing to drink.

If they do come around, remember to praise their efforts—even if it wasn't in *your* time frame.

Procrastination

Once tasks are properly assigned—the ones you will be responsible for and those given to others—next on the agenda is *getting them done*. If we know what we have to do, why do so many of us procrastinate? It goes deeper than just being lazy. Our fear may be surfacing again. Sometimes we don't complete a task because we are afraid of failing or we don't feel entitled to succeed. For instance, you put off a job search because inwardly you believe you're not worthy of having a better position. Or on the flip side, you may be fearful that you will actually succeed at the task, which would bring about a whole new set of challenges.

Waiting until the last minute to undertake projects forces you to maintain an unhealthy crash-and-burn working style. And you pay a steep price for this, namely, *your sanity*. Remember, you can be afraid and take action anyway.

Here are some strategies to help you move forward:

- When confronted by a task that seems over-whelming, break it down into several actions with a timetable of when you will perform each one.
- As you achieve each action, acknowledge what you've done. This may seem insignificant, but it isn't. It will give you momentum to do more.
- Set up a simple reward system for when you complete each action. Do something nice for yourself—for example, take a walk, call a friend, etc.

Another way to tackle procrastination is to prepare for the task at hand. This sets the groundwork for getting the job done. For example, if you need to update your resume, first make a list of your latest accomplishments, next put your old resume near the computer, then go out and buy bond paper stock. And splurge on the expensive paper if it will get you excited about the process.

Petty Grievances

It's easy to get caught up in these: a loved one speaking in a harsh tone, a child making his twentieth demand of the hour, a friend overlooking a special invitation. When these things come up (and they always do), they can either continue to irritate us or we can take action to let people know how we feel (if appropriate) and then move on. If we focus on how others have "wronged" us and exaggerate their behavior, we are wasting precious energy that can be put to better use. The choice is ours.

Next time something happens that irritates you, and you are holding on to it, ask yourself: *How important is the incident when compared to what I truly value?* Isn't it more important to have satisfying relationships with family and friends than to dwell on minor irritations?

Exercise: The 60-Second Inventory

Use the 60-second inventory during the day. It can help you identify how you are feeling and irritations that may be bothering you. Here's what you do. *Pause* several times during the day for a reality check, and ask yourself:

1. *What am I feeling?* Actually pinpoint the feeling, such as being angry with your boss for not acknowledging the overtime hours you've put in lately, or being jealous of a friend who always seems to carve out time for a vacation, when you don't. If you have trouble identifying your feelings, call a friend and share what's happening. She may be able to help.

2. *How am I holding on?* You've identified what's bothering you, and maybe it's appropriate to take an action, like telling your friend, "I'm disappointed that you forgot about my dinner party." But once you do

this, let it go. Look at the consequence. If you don't, it zaps your energy so that you can't create what you truly want for yourself.

3. *What am I grateful for in this moment?* To complete the letting-go process, reflect on what you have to be grateful for, right now. If you can't think of anything, make it up. Act as if there are a lot of things. (You know what will happen? That will become true for you.)

Gossip

Just don't do it! It's an energy drainer and by engaging in it, you are likely putting off something you need to be doing right now. Yes, sometimes juicy tidbits are great to chew on, but they lose their taste quickly. When you are with friends who start to gossip, don't encourage them by joining in. You'll feel better about yourself as a result.

Step Three: Please Yourself

ow that you have looked at habits that don't serve you anymore and have the tools to let them go, you are ready to take action to bring more pleasure into your life. Step Three focuses on your spiritual renewal—taking time for yourself. Let's start by exploring the nature of play.

As children, we create ways of having fun all the time. But unfortunately, as adults, many of us lose our ability to play. We feel overly responsible for others; relegating *our* "playtime" to the back burner. And we wonder why our lives feel mechanical and uninteresting.

Everyday Pleasures

In order to have fun and recharge, you don't have to go away for a long weekend or take time off from work. All you need is a few minutes a day to reconnect with the things that make you joyful.

If you've lost touch with these, keep tabs on activities you look forward to, like calling a friend for no reason, splurging on a special dessert, taking a lipstick or hand cream break, or picking up a book that you think you'll never have time to read—and actually starting it.

Need some help coming up with things? The list below contains everyday pleasures from a survey of working women that we conducted for this book:

- Write to a friend you've lost contact with.
- Laugh with your child and allow yourself to be silly.
- Take quiet time. Sit in a comfortable chair for at least five to ten minutes.
- Give yourself a foot massage.
- Take a walk in a natural setting.
- Visit a jazz bar and let the music soothe your soul.
- Take a bath with a luxurious bubble mixture.
- Read a chapter of your favorite book.
- Knit, sew, crochet, or cross-stitch something for you or your home.
- Allow yourself to take a long glance at the latest styles in your favorite boutique.

- Get the crayons out and buy yourself a coloring book. Then go to it.
- Play a hand of jacks or any other children's game that you delight in.
- Listen to some relaxing music.
- Rent a favorite movie and watch it either alone or with a friend.
- Meditate.

I'd like you to write down ways to pamper yourself this week and make a commitment to follow through:

Action 1

_____

_____

_____

_____

Action 2

_____

_____

_____

_____

Being gracious with yourself is like anything new you undertake, it takes practice, patience, and persistence. Naturally, pangs of guilt will start to surface as you are nicer to yourself. Pay no attention to them. It's par for the course!

Claim Your Passion

Now, what turns you on? What gets the blood racing in your veins? What are you passionate about? Think back to college, high school, even childhood—what were the things that excited you? Was it something that one of your friends was pursuing but you were too afraid to try yourself? It could be anything—acting, scuba diving, flower arranging, volunteering at a local shelter, teaching teenagers English. The list goes on.

If you are able to answer these questions, then move on to the questionnaire that follows the exercises. If you're having trouble thinking of something you'd like to bring into your life, try one of the following exercises.

Exercise: Inner Reflection

Find a place where you feel comfortable, like a favorite chair in your living room or a quiet spot outdoors. Go there and close your eyes. Then, take a few deep breaths. Don't pay attention to the thoughts that are vying for your attention.

Once you begin to relax, ask yourself: *What do I yearn to do that I haven't done in a long time?* Then listen to your heart answering the call. You will know what you've been neglecting.

Exercise: Writing

If inner reflection isn't generating any ideas about your passions, you may want to try stream of consciousness writing. Just grab paper and a pen and write without thinking. Set a timer for five or ten minutes and see what you come up with.

Don't stop; if you get stuck, write the same word over and over until you move out of your rut. Many people feel uncomfortable the first time they try this type of writing, but with practice it can help you reach another level of awareness.

Questionnaire

1. I am passionate about… (finish this sentence below).

_____

_____

_____

_____

2. How have you nurtured your passion recently or in the past, through a hobby or some work-related interest?

_____

_____

_____

3. What actions can you commit to this month to help you pursue or continue to pursue an activity you feel passionate about?

_____

_____

_____

_____

_____

_____

_____

_____

_____

When you bring a new activity into your life, do it one step at a time. If you were training for a marathon, you'd start with a mile and work your way up. The same is true for what you feel passionate about. If you want to paint, start by buying a set of oils, an easel, and some brushes. Experiment for a while and get back into the flow of the work. Then when you feel ready, sign up for a class.

As you begin to make room for what you love, you may feel some resistance coming up, thinking, *I'm being selfish* or *I've started too late and wasted too much time.* It's important that you don't listen to this chatter. Just keep moving forward and pay attention to your heart's calling.

Step Four: Flex Your "Inner" Muscles

As with any muscle, your "inner" muscles—the ones that make you joyful—must be exercised regularly. Their upkeep is simple. You need to make a conscious effort each day to think positively. The reflections on the next page will help you do that. Pick one and say it to yourself at different times during the day (for example, on your commute, at lunch, etc.). Call a friend and share it with her. If it helps, write it down on notes to post around your home or on your computer, or write it in a journal, or in your Sparkle Log at the end of this book.

There are enough reflections to last you two weeks if you choose to rotate them on a daily basis. After that time, either start the sequence again or make up your own. If you find one that is particularly meaningful, stick with it for a few days or a week.

Inner Upkeep

1. I create new ways of playing and carve out the time to do so.
2. I look at my surroundings as if I were seeing them for the first time.
3. I allow the excitement of change to fill my life.
4. I will not "react" to situations that cause me stress. Instead, I will observe what is going on.
5. I take good care of myself by doing at least one thing just for me today.
6. I use humor in all my affairs.
7. I am exactly where I am supposed to be.
8. I have enough time and energy to do what's needed today.
9. I look at the people in my life as if I'm meeting them for the first time.
10. I make loving choices for myself.
11. I let go of old habits, and watch my life unfold.
12. I stop rehashing worst-case scenarios.
13. I see the potential in situations before me.
14. My words serve to create kindness around me.

Quiet Time

Often we get caught up in the rush of an activity, feeling as if there's never enough time to do what we have to. Thinking this way only creates greater frenzy and a self-fulfilling prophecy. We end up *not* having enough time. It's useful to stop whatever you're doing when a never-enough-time attack comes on and *pause* for a moment.

Exercise: Permission to Rest

Sit in a comfortable chair and let your eyes close. Breathe deeply. As thoughts enter your mind, just note them. Continue breathing deeply. Now, listen to the sounds around you. Pinpoint the closest sound, the furthest sound. Keep listening. Tell yourself: *It's my time to relax.* Practice this each day for about three minutes.

We are so used to doing
for others that when we have
a moment of free time,
we may feel guilty and
not take it for ourselves.

Give yourself permission
to rest and enjoy your
quiet time.

Humor

It's the great equalizer. It can diffuse stress and make us look on the brighter side. We need to get into the habit of using it when we start taking ourselves too seriously.

Exercise: Pretend Laughter

After a long day or when you are in a bad mood, try laughing. Even if you can't find anything to laugh about, make yourself laugh—the louder the better. It feels silly at first; however, it will ultimately make you feel good. But if tricking yourself into happiness isn't working for you, then at least the image of how ridiculous you look laughing at nothing will bring a genuine smile to your face.

Carve Out "She" Time

Haven't gotten together with friends lately? Don't wait any longer—initiate the calls and set it up.

Women find solace and rejuvenation in the company of other women. Of course, getting together is the best source of renewal, but receiving caring emails works wonders between visits.

Schedule a Retreat

Whether going yourself or with a friend, make your plans. You deserve it! There are several websites that list retreat centers and spas across the country. These facilities will vary in price for a weekend stay. To keep costs down, some will offer packages. Be sure to ask for them. Enjoy your research. Know that there is a wonderful place just waiting for you to visit.

Don't Go It Alone!

For more information check out our website www.womenworking2000.com. You'll find strategies from women on navigating work/life, advancement, and leadership, as well as power networking contacts, helpful books, and much more.

Sparkle Log

he pages that follow enable you to jot down actions that will make the simple wisdom contained in this book a part of your everyday life. I suggest that you fill them out right after you finish reading. You can always come back to them and add other insights later on.

Be More, Not Do More

How will you incorporate resting, reflecting, and spending time with yourself in your daily routine? Jot down some actions you intend to take.

Saying "No" Is Like Saying "Yes" to Yourself

Jot down some things you don't want to do anymore. Make a point to say "no" the next time you are asked to do them. Call a friend for support if you need to.

_____

_____

_____

_____

_____

_____

_____

_____

Don't Take It Personally

Write down statements you can tell yourself the next time you are criticized and feel like reacting. Remember—it probably has nothing to do with you!

_____

_____

_____

_____

_____

_____

_____

Live in the Grays of Life

Trying to be "perfect" robs you of living joyously. Jot down times when you feel yourself becoming rigid or a bit compulsive because you're attempting to do something "exactly right." Note the physical sensations in your body when this occurs (for example, tightness in the throat and shortness of breath). Becoming aware of your reactions will help you change them.

_____

_____

_____

_____

_____

_____

Sparkle Sustainers

ake this list of Sparkle Sustainers and make a copy of it. Place it where you can see it at home and at the office. I want you to glance at these simple sayings throughout the day and be sure to read the whole list when you are feeling particularly stretched. The wisdom here is applicable to most situations you will be confronted with.

- Speak out on issues you feel passionate about.

- Don't procrastinate, just do it!

- When you feel yourself tensing up, *breathe deeply*.

- What you can change, change. What you can't, leave alone—let go!

- When you make a mistake, don't dwell on it. Move on—*next*!

- When you receive criticism, take what fits, and leave the rest.

- When you are about to criticize someone, *stop*. Look at what's bothering you!

- Before you act in a way you will regret—*think*.

- Don't force solutions—answers will evolve in their proper time.

- When disputes arise, look for the common ground—it's there.

- Offer praise like it is going out of style.

In this book, you have been given the tools to maintain your sparkle. Now use them with confidence to bring more joy into your life. Join the many women who are chanting a new mantra, *Time for Me*.

About the Author

Helene Lerner hosts Emmy Award–winning programs on public television that cover a wide range of topics affecting women today. A former columnist for *New Woman* magazine and for the *New York Post's* "Wellness Watch," she also has authored several books, including *Embrace Change, Finding Balance, Stress Breakers*, and *Our Power As Women: Wisdom and Strategies of Highly Successful Women*.

Helene is the founder of the popular website www.womenworking2000.com, which features success strategies for navigating work/life, advancement, and leadership; power-networking contacts; book recommendations; and more. She maintains a private practice coaching individuals and groups on self-mastery and power, balancing career and family, creating mentoring and networking partnerships, stress reduction, and other health issues.

Her company, Creative Expansions, Inc. (CEI), is designed to help women actualize their potential, and she consults with *Fortune* 500 companies on diversity issues. A member of Phi Beta Kappa, she holds a master's degree in education and an MBA in management sciences.

Helene is available for keynotes, seminars, and coaching. Contact her via email at: helene@womenworking2000.com.

For more information on purchasing copies of Helene's television programs, go to: www.womenworking2000.com/lerner/docs/ helene_tv.html

60-minute women's forums/videocassettes

Make It Happen: Mentors, Dreams, Success

Women Going Global

Rocking the Barriers

Women Working 2000 and Beyond

30-minute documentaries

Fathers and Daughters: Journeys of the Heart

Heartbeat to Heartbeat: Women and Heart Disease

Pure Magic: The Mother-Daughter Bond
winner of a 2005 Gracie Award from American Women
in Radio and Television

Phenomenal Voyage: Women and Technology

Choices over a Lifetime

Proud to Be a Girl
winner of a 2004 New York Emmy Award

Grab Hold of the Reins: Women and Cancer
winner of a 2003 Gracie Award from American Women
in Radio and Television

Blazes of Light: Women Living with HIV/AIDS
an Emmy nominee and winner of a 2000 Gracie Award
from American Women in Radio and Television

Osteoporosis: Breaking the Fall

Osteoporosis: Your Bones, Your Life
winner of a 1997 National Media Owl Award from the
Retirement Research Foundation

Finding the Strength Within: Living with Cancer

Out of the Darkness: Women and Depression
winner of a 1999 New York Emmy Award and winner
of a 1999 Gracie Award from American Women in
Radio and Television

Alzheimer's Disease: Descent into Silence

Courageous Portraits: Living with Cancer